The HARLEM GLOBETROTTERS

America's *Favorite* Basketball Team

by Alice Cary
illustrated by Bob Dorsey

Scott Foresman

Editorial Offices: Glenview, Illinois • New York, New York
Sales Offices: Reading, Massachusetts • Duluth, Georgia
Glenview, Illinois • Carrollton, Texas • Menlo Park, California

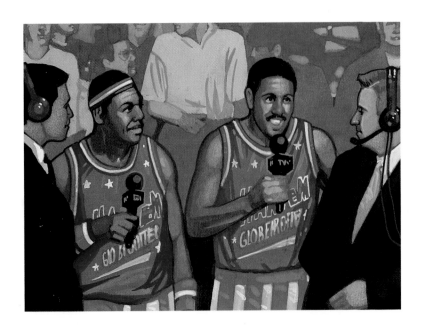

January 12, 1998, was a big day in Remington, Indiana. Cars jammed the high school parking lot. People crowded into the gym. Reporters and TV cameras waited. A letter from President Clinton waited too!

The star basketball team took the court. On this day, the Harlem Globetrotters would play their twenty thousandth game. The crowd went wild.

No other professional sports team had ever played so many games. The Globetrotters had played before more people, and in more places, than any other team in the world.

This time the Globetrotters played the New York Nationals. As usual, the Globetrotters dazzled the crowd. They handled the ball like magic. They performed amazing tricks. As always, their fans laughed and cheered.

The Globetrotters beat the Nationals 85–62. In seventy-two seasons, the Globetrotters had attained a tremendous record of 19,668 wins. They had lost only 332 times.

"This is our New Year's Eve, our birthday, our July Fourth, our anniversary, all rolled into one," said the team's owner.

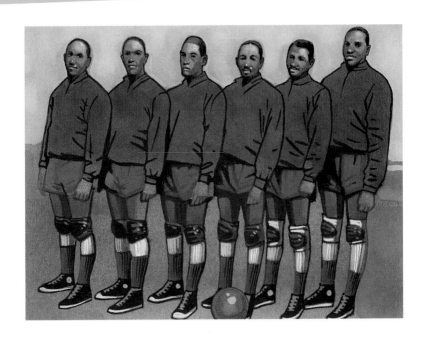

How did this tremendous team get its start? Their story is one of dedication in the face of racial injustice.

Basketball began in 1891. But the National Basketball Association (NBA) didn't include African American players until 1950. That didn't stop the Globetrotters, though. They began as an African American team in the 1920s.

Now, years later, most people have heard of the Harlem Globetrotters. But few know that they aren't from Harlem. They never were. And the team almost stopped playing soon after it was formed.

The story began in Chicago in 1926. Twenty-four-year-old Abe Saperstein organized a team of African American basketball players. He called them the "Savoy Big Five."

The Savoy was a famous ballroom. Its owners wanted more business. They invited the new team to play there. They hoped people would watch the game and then stay to dance. But the plan didn't work. The games ended. So much for the team.

Saperstein decided to take some of his players on the road. They all crowded into his Model-T Ford. They wore uniforms that said "New York" on them. People thought that's where they were from.

The team played its first game in Hinckley, Illinois, on January 7, 1927. A crowd of three hundred people showed up.

The players continued to tour the Midwest. In 1930, they changed their name to the Harlem Globetrotters. Harlem was an area in New York City where many African Americans lived. The Globetrotters wanted everyone to know that they were African American. They wanted to do their part to stop racial injustice. And they were globetrotters—they traveled all over.

The Globetrotters won game after game. They traveled to new places every year. More and more people came to see them.

During one game in 1939, the team was ahead 112 to 5. One of the players grew bored. He began to clown around. The crowd loved his tricks.

After the game, Saperstein told his team they could continue to joke during games, but only if they were well ahead of the other team. Dedication and hard work came first, after all.

A few years later, Reece "Goose" Tatum joined the team. He was a super basketball player and a born comedian. He invented tricks and pranks that made the Globetrotters even more famous.

n 1939, the Globetrotters suffered a minor disaster. In their first professional championship, they lost to another African American team, the New York Rens. The Rens went on to win the championship.

The next year, however, the Globetrotters gave the Rens a jolt. They beat them during another championship. Then they beat the Chicago Bruins in overtime, 31–29. Now the Globetrotters were the World Basketball Champions.

When they returned to Chicago after the championship, 22,000 people turned out to watch them play.

More and more people wanted to see the Harlem Globetrotters in action. *Life* magazine featured an article about them in 1946. Movies were made about their lives.

The team players began to travel overseas. Now they were truly globetrotters. They went to Hawaii, Europe, and South America. Even the pope wanted to see them. Once they even played on the deck of a United States aircraft carrier.

The team became so popular that it stopped battles. In 1956, Peru was in the middle of a civil war. But everyone stopped fighting for four days to watch the Harlem Globetrotters. As soon as the team left, the war resumed.

In one place, however, the crowd didn't cheer. The audience was absolutely quiet.

In 1949, the Globetrotters became the first professional basketball team to tour Alaska. They traveled by dog sled to play before a group of Inuits.

They played well. They did their usual stunts. But the Inuits didn't laugh. They didn't clap. The crowd was silent.

Later the Globetrotters learned an interesting thing about the Inuit culture. When Inuits are quiet, they really like the show.

At one point, the team had a serious problem. The players were so good that other teams didn't want to play them.

Team owner Abe Saperstein knew just what to do. He talked to his friend, Louis "Red" Klotz. He convinced Klotz to organize some new teams for the Globetrotters to play against.

Klotz did just that. His new teams included the Washington Generals, the Boston Shamrocks, and the Baltimore Rockets. Now the Globetrotters would be busy.

Over the years, some interesting players joined the Globetrotters. Two famous team "clowns" were George "Meadowlark" Lemon and "Curley" Neal. They made people laugh everywhere they went.

Wilt "The Stilt" Chamberlain joined the team in 1958. Some say he was basketball's greatest offensive player ever. He stayed with the team one year, and then joined the NBA.

The first woman joined the team in 1985. Expert ball handler Lynette Woodard played for several seasons. Then she joined a team in Italy.

In 1997, team members Michael "Wild Thing" Wilson and Fred "Preacher" Smith set a new basketball world record. In England, they made a slam dunk of eleven feet, eleven inches!

Abe Saperstein died in 1966, at age sixty-three. He had been a tremendous leader. In forty years, he had taken his players to twelve hundred cities and eighty-two foreign countries. They had played nearly 8,945 games, with only 330 losses. Best of all, his players made people smile. No wonder everyone loved the Globetrotters.

The team's fame continued to grow. In 1970 a TV cartoon series called *The Harlem Globetrotters Show* began. It was a big hit. This was the first time a sports team had such a show on TV.

It seemed as if everyone wanted to be part of the act. When the leader of China visited the United States in 1979, he asked to meet the Globetrotters.

In 1982, the Globetrotters got their own star on Hollywood's Walk of Fame. Once again, they were the only sports team to receive such an honor.

I n 1996, the team was seventy years old. To celebrate, they decided to do something very special.

The Globetrotters went to South Africa. There had been racial problems there for years. Now, though, South Africa was working out many of these problems and moving closer to racial equality. The Globetrotters were the first professional basketball team to play in the new South Africa. They raised over a million dollars to help children there.

A year later the Globetrotters were invited to return to South Africa. President Nelson Mandela was having his seventy-ninth birthday party.

The Globetrotters and Mandela were good partners. Both had spent years dedicating themselves to stamping out racial injustice.

Over the years, the Globetrotters have proved that they are indeed America's favorite basketball team.